WORLD WITHOUT

BY THE SAME AUTHOR

In Daylight (Printed Matter, 1995)
Monumenta Nipponica (Saru, 1995)
The Painting Stick (Pine Wave, 2005)
From the Japanese (Isobar, 2013)

WORLD WITHOUT

PAUL ROSSITER

ISOBAR
PRESS

First published in 2015 by

Isobar Press
Sakura 2-21-23-202, Setagaya-ku,
Tokyo 156-0053, Japan
&
14 Isokon Flats, Lawn Road,
London NW3 2XD, United Kingdom

http://isobarpress.com

ISBN 978-4-907359-13-3

ACKNOWLEDGEMENTS

Some of these poems were first published in
NOON: *journal of the short poem, Tears in the Fence* and *Tokyo
Poetry Journal;* 'Reading Philip Whalen' appeared online in
A Festschrift for Tony Frazer, edited by Richard Berengarten,
Aidan Semmens and others. My thanks to all these editors.

COVER IMAGE
James Turrell, *Deer Shelter Skyspace,* 2006. An Art Fund
Commission. Courtesy of the artist and Yorkshire Sculpture Park.
Photograph by Paul Rossiter.

CONTENTS

I

world without

II

landscapes

III

found in transcription

IV

ars longa

V

white foxglove

for Maya

I

world without

LISTENING TO JAZZ ALL DAY

Hemphill, Lake, Bluiett & Murray (wsq)
bathing the soul
in the juice of four squeezed saxophones

spiky and astringent, Monk
constructing a new
and asymmetrical architecture of the ear

Bill Frisell (Mr Pedals) and his Telecaster
conjuring
a phantasmagoria of resonances out of air

genres float through the room
like large benign ghosts

       I have no idea what will happen next

Gil Evans:
'insecurity is the secret of eternal youth'

WEATHERING

storm pulses in from the Pacific
jolts of lightning, explosive thunder
trees thrash high above the roof in darkness

half a mile away
rain pelts down on Gōtokuji temple and graveyard
(300 *lords, wives, concubines and children of the Clan of Ii*)

splashing onto
and sluicing off
the Buddha Hall's steep-pitched copper roof

as it has nights like this
for over three hundred years
(wet earth, leaning stones and rain-soaked moss)

Reading Philip Whalen

who follows
the thread while
letting all manner of things intrude to

    deflect the flow, to
    get included, to be annotated, to
    scatter yet sharpen the attention

wasp on the window-pane
ideas that happen to happen through the door
small outbursts of entertainment vaudeville burlesque
acted out in the theatre of the skull

'all over the place …'
but always going forward

    a graph of a mind moving …

and even if the grin is a bit fixed

    ('that nice, that clever Mr Whalen!')

the voice nevertheless goes on
    in the words of the enthusiastic Mr McClure
being 'mock-serious, biting, casual
good-natured, concise, powerful, and humorous'

    (did you remember to bring the gin?)

WATCHING BIRDS EAT

mejiro, or white-eyes

would come from their nests to feed
each other berries
from the tree outside our window
each June

but since our neighbour chopped down
his patch of bamboo to
enhance the value of his land

not a single one

(bulbuls steal the berries out of each others' beaks)

Remembering Lol Coxhill

a gathering of England's musical avant-garde
white beards everywhere
good lord, wonderful to see you, are you still alive?

scratchy radio static
intermittent drum-beats and cymbal-scraping

a power trio disassembles Hendrix

multiphonic altissimo saxophone drone and flutter

a guitar played with a bow
a violin strummed like a guitar
a singer with his hat made from a cabbage

      professionally amateur
      straight-faced, hilarious, earnest, spiky

gathered together
in a late-imperial, wood-panelled, high-ceilinged hall
with long purple drapes drawn across the windows

to commemorate
a lifetime of commitment to the instant

the passionate, generous
and slightly mad engagement with sound
of one of their own

LISTENING TO THE WALLPAPER

red plastic bench seats
low lighting and fake marble tables
smooth-jazz Muzak
        (it's painless and you won't hear a thing)
paintings of cattle wading into Highland streams
portions of said cattle at £20 a chunk

and then, suddenly, on the speakers
Ella Fitzgerald is singing *Night and Day*
voice dancing on tiptoe
        through the changes, through the lyrics
inventing all the notes she needs
to create the world she hears the music making

        1956, thirty-nine years old, at once

a young girl's voice still full of yearning
and the grown woman's full-fledged song
replete with knowledge, style, poise and joy

marble pillars, mosaic floor
looped calligraphy on peacock-blue tiles

> *He has created man and taught him speech*
> *He has set the sun and moon in their courses*

a square pond with a trickling fountain
plump diwan cushions
a stuffed peacock
blue-and-white ceramic jars
a stained-glass window with
      a carved and gilded cedar-wood frame
inlaid Egyptian woodwork
gilded ceiling, Ottoman chandelier

a *mashrabiyah* (lattice-work upper-storey window) creating
a *zenana*, a space for modestly peeking women

> Kashan, Damascus, Iznik
> Sind, Kubachi, Cairo, Istanbul

thank you very much, Frederic, Lord Leighton (1830–1896)

as we step out into the twenty-first-century rain
falling steadily on Holland Park Road, London W14

mother of all temples and shrines
a *grande dame* who's seen a bit in her time
      Athene, Virgin Mary, mosque, powder store
      Venetian artillery, Lord Elgin, UNESCO
floodlit now in all her ruination
a crone with gap-toothed colonnades and fallen pediments

taramosalata, olives, anchovies, butter beans, roast chicken
robust red wine
photograph (1948) of Seferis and Katsimbalis on the wall
black pouches under Seferis's eyes

morning, fourth-floor balcony
blue railings, blue awnings, a blue-and-white flag
sun warms my knees
thick yoghurt with honey and nuts, hard-boiled egg
bread and jam and excellent coffee

      you want a traditional Greek breakfast?
      this isn't it?
      oh no! two cups of coffee and five cigarettes

WAITER: *if I had a gun I'd be in prison now*
those politicians in the parliament
they don't even dare go to the window to look out
they and all those other big people stole all the money
and now it's in Latin America somewhere or Switzerland

RECEPTIONIST: *it's no use*
thinking about what happened, we need to think about what's next
so calm yourself

a demonstration assembles
coaches park in side streets
marchers bussed in from all over the country
      FOR BANK$ BAILING OUT PEOPLE GOT SOLD OUT !!!
scooters and motorbikes with horns sounding
      WALK IN SOLIDARITY
thousands on foot led by drums, banners and loud-hailers
applauded from the pavements as they pass

shutters, padlocks and FOR RENT signs
      the arcades are empty
plastic bags blow across marble floors in the shadows

old men sit on straight-backed chairs at the roadside
orange trees line the streets
      dark green foliage full of fruit
men with their hats on gesticulate in cafés
a tiny white-haired woman tends the lamps in a chapel

Kalamata olives, hummus, beetroot salad, cod with garlic puré
robust red wine
a photo of the owner's uncle, killed in Albania, 1940

      written on a wall in Plaka:
      THERE ARE TWO RULES FOR SUCCESS:
      1. NEVER TELL EVERYTHING YOU KNOW.

Archaeological Museum
'Mask of Agamemnon'

      shock of shining gold verisimilitude

21–24 *November* 2012

Passing Time

the sun wheels across the southern sky
and the room that –
       it seems only a moment ago –
was full of light is now in shadow

and we're all that much nearer
       our one irrevocable end
and nothing
of much import has been achieved

Artie the cat
inspects his left forepaw for about a minute
licks it twice
then takes a nap

CROSSING THE THESSALIAN PLAIN

abandoned car dealerships
unfinished houses
the concrete shell of a mall
bunches of steel spikes bristling from concrete roofs
crushed cars
and discarded machines
share green fields with imperturbably ruminant goats

engraved shields, helmets, breast-plates
swords, axes, steel headpieces for horses
cross-bows, halberds with six-foot shafts
quivers of steel-tipped arrows
twelve-foot pike-shafts tufted with small red tassels
arquebuses with engraved hexagonal barrels

a chastity belt (late fifteenth century?)
with steel-fanged anus and vulva

the museum of the Palazzo Ducale

> welcome to the Venice Jazz Club!
> our location: S. Barnaba, Ponte dei Pugni (the Bridge of Fists)
> *from September to Christmas each year*
> *rival clans would gather at bridges without rails*
> *and throw punches with the goal of knocking opponents*
> *into the cold and sewage-strewn canal below*
> *this was tolerated by the Council of Ten*
> *as it marked a big improvement over the earlier tradition*
> *of fights with sharpened and fire-hardened sticks*

Office of the Heads of the Council of Ten
(*no one – not even the accused – may enter the room during a trial*)
in the antechamber a *Bocca di Leone* (Lion's Mouth)
          for the deposit of denunciations
next door the State Inquisitors' office
next to that the torture chamber
and so at last to the prisons

BEING IN TUNE

Stan Tracey
in dark overcoat, rumpled suit and Hush Puppies
as of tonight (29th December 2012)
eighty-six-years-minus-one-day old

    ('somewhere deep inside the crusty old cynicism'
    he once said
    'is still the bright-eyed lad thinking, *hey this is great!*')

sits down at the piano in the Bull's Head and plays
the particular out-of-tune note (*ouch!*)
he remembers from last month's gig, looks up and remarks

time changes nothing

RECOMMENDING TRISTANO

for Dorsey Kleitz

an email from Dorsey:

> A quick question. Lennie Tristano? I've been reading *The Lonely Voice of Jack Kerouac* where it mentions Tristano was one of Kerouac's favorite jazz pianists. I've never heard of him. Any recommendations, must listens?

flawless technique
perfectly even articulation
underlying steady eighth-note feel
emotionally cool
        (though a much tougher cool than cool-school cool)
structural rigour
a great teacher, the first to teach jazz in a systematic way
influential not only on piano players –
        ladies and gentlemen, please welcome
        Lee Konitz on alto! Warne Marsh on tenor! –
first to record free group improvisations –
        ('Intuition', 'Digression', 1949)
first to use overdubbing, multi-tracking and
        post-production changes of tape-speed

        if Charlie Parker is the Schoenberg
        of modern jazz, then Tristano is its Webern
            (Cook & Morton)

following
the path of rhythmic strictness with formidable exactitude

long, angular strings of
almost even eighth-notes provided with
subtle rhythmic deviations and abrasive polytonal effects

a living equilibrium between
forward drive and polyrhythmically-based accenting

Tristano (Atlantic, 1955)
The New Tristano (Atlantic, 1961)

on most of the tracks he works with
multiple times
setting 5/4 or 3/8 or some other time against a steady 4/4
and producing astonishing contours made up of, say

4 on 3 (in one hand)
on top of 5 on 4 (in the other hand)
on top of 4/4 (the basic beat)

what I care about is that the result sounded good to me

I can never think and play at the same time – it's an emotional
                                                    impossibility

KNOWING ONE'S PLACE

walk, early morning, through the neighbourhood
three-bed housing, balconied mansion blocks
a small agricultural plot sown with cabbages
follow the line of cherry trees that follows
the course of the concrete-covered river

> *hiyodori* (bulbuls) shriek, *suzume* (sparrows) chirp
> *mejiro* (white-eyes) flit in and out of bushes

to Setagaya Hachiman shrine
founded by Minamoto no Yoshiie (Shogun) in 1091

'the god of eight banners' – of warriors, war, and archery

> square vermilion pillars, horned gables
> curved roofs of overlapping copper tiles
> wind-bells tinkle at the eaves

renovated in 1546
by Kira Yoriyasu, lord of Setagaya

> swept gravel precinct
> *kuromatsu, kashi, kaya, keyaki*
> black pine, evergreen oak, nutmeg, zelkova

> *chikaraishi*, 'strength-stones', says the sign:

> > river boulders
> > nested like eggs on a bed of white gravel
> > each engraved with the stone's weight
> > and the name of the man who had lifted it

an intense-looking high-school boy
mounts the granite steps to the shrine
bows and claps – and prays and prays and prays

out, past bakery and beauty parlour
      (a satchelled schoolgirl runs by, late for class)
past convenience store, second-hand clothes shop
      (a woman waters her wall-top potted plants)
across steel tracks laid on weedy ballast
      (a bent old woman sweeps her doorstep)
skirting an antique tram preserved for kids to play in

to the avenue of leaning pines that leads to the gate
of Gōtokuji (Zen temple, Sōtō sect)
founded by Kira Masatada
in memory of his aunt, who died in 1480

      three gilded statues
      seated in the shadowy Buddha Hall

the Kira clan defeated by Toyotomi Hideyoshi,
and their castle (just down the road) destroyed, in 1590

      a leafy mound, dry moat
      park benches and public toilets
      cicadas shrilling in the summer heat

most of Setagaya given
to the Ii clan by Tokugawa Ieyasu
for services rendered by Ii Naomasa
      and his 3,600 troops in crimson armour ('Red Devils')
at the battle of Sekigahara (1600)

Gōtokuji thereafter the family temple of the Ii

    eaves, roof-beams, water-tubs
    their crest is everywhere

buried here is Ii Naosuke who
on the deck of the uss Powhatan
signed the 'Treaty of Amity and Commerce' (1858)
    (co-signatory: Commodore Townsend Harris)
and who for his pains was cut down by seventeen samurai
at the Sakurada Gate of the Imperial Palace
24 March 1860

    a column on a carved lotus-flower base
    in a stone enclosure
    stone fence-posts, stone doors, the entrance flanked
    by stone lanterns capped with moss

a metal plaque gives the details of his story
his grave still frequently visited

KNOWING ONE'S PLACE: PART 2

Setagaya: forty-two villages
rice paddies
wheat, millet, cotton, hemp, sweet potato fields
oranges, mulberry, tea, bamboo

labour in the fields in summer
make straw boots and cloaks in winter
plait straw ropes, mend clothes, pound rice

cotton kimonos, loin cloths, straw sandals

the annual tax collector's visit
            (land tax 40–50% of the harvest)
taxes on doors, windows, female children
cloth, saké, hazel trees, beans and hemp

sesame seeds and peasants are very much alike
the more you squeeze them the more you can extract from them

insect damage, drought, typhoon

if a farmer leaves his field, either to engage in trade, or to work
for hire, not only must he be punished, but the whole village
must be indicted with him – Hideyoshi (1591)

husbands hold the family seal
wives the rice scooper

no family names to start with
none of their given names now known

Visiting the Ancestors

I

sea-wind, a red-tiled path beside
      a semicircle of sandy beach
slanting shadows in early evening sunlight
boats coming in and out of Kobe
an early-Taisho-Era green-painted octagonal villa
with sage-green shutters and steep Dutch-gabled roof
      (now the Sun Yat Sen Memorial Hall)
its eccentric elegance dwarfed
      by the 300-metre-high concrete towers
of the bridge across the strait to Awaji-shima

we take Maya's gentle eighty-three-year-old father
      (ex-merchant seaman, communist, Esperanto enthusiast)
for a gentle spin along the sea-front in his wheelchair
      (cancer, two strokes, heart attack, but he still keeps going)
he points left and says *turn right*
he points right and says *turn left*
he points straight ahead and says
      my head isn't working properly any more

2

okonomiyaki restaurant where we're the only customers
and where the owner
        sixty-two years old and still a beauty
has been hitting the *shōchū* cocktails –
almost too drunk to cook, but she manages in the end
after frequent reminders about what we'd ordered

she talks a lot, switching between
Japanese and lightly inflected NHK-acquired English
        I wanted to learn it because
        when I was at junior high I used to wonder if I was a half
and occasionally breaks into short sequences
of sexy dance-steps
        spatulas held high like handkerchiefs or castanets
as she shimmies behind the sizzling hot-plate

she won't let us pay for our drinks because
she's had such a good time, and because
she well remembers Maya's favourite aunt
who, thirty years ago, kept the sweetshop down the road

3

waterside hotel, grey morning
bull-rushes, sedge
rain-drops winking rings on the water's surface
electric-blue flash of a kingfisher low across the pond

4

Suma, where
after the defeat of the Heike in 1184
the flute player Taira no Atsumori
sixteen or seventeen years old
  with a lightly powdered face and blackened teeth
was killed on the beach
  (a boy just the age of his own son)
by Kumagai Naozane

a haiku by Bashō inscribed on a stone
in the temple garden:

>   *oh, Suma-dera*
>   *listening to the no-sound of the flute*
>   *in the darkness under the trees*

and another by Buson:

>   *the waves*
>   *attracted by the sound of the flute –*
>   *Suma in autumn*

the flute itself is in the temple's treasure house

5

remove withered stalks from the vases
replace them with green *sakaki*, refresh the water
light incense sticks, pour water over the stone
never ask the ancestors for anything, just thank them

grandfather, third son of a landowner
fell in love with a geisha
married her and was disinherited
fathered twelve children then died of a stroke at forty
Ryōichi, the eldest son, took over the father's role
called up in 1942
he sent his mother letters from wherever he was posted

a 500 lb. bomb
straight through the steel-plate deck
of a troop transport en route for Manila

for the rest of her life
periodically
she locked herself away and re-read all his letters

which were cremated with her, their ash
mingled with hers under the stone

pour more water
over the smooth wet shining granite

6

train back to Tokyo
look up to see
rows of pre-fabricated houses straddling a hillside
their windows looking down
      on flooded paddy fields and
the white flash of our Shinkansen racing between two tunnels

Looking at The City from Parliament Hill

1

a kestrel wheels and hovers
    above rough grass and woodland
a siren's wail floats up from Kentish Town
a retriever noses scents through tangled bushes

against a hazy pearl-grey sky
    stained citron at the eastern horizon
the skyline of Canary Wharf and the City
a double-peaked bar-graph, illustrating
    a nasty recession between two chunky booms

    look, son
    that's where the money lives and breeds

assets, ambitions, anxiety, algorithms
fermenting in their steel and glass housings

2

when the call comes people know right away: we may use
the most innocent tone of voice when we say: 'hi, could you
pop up to the 20th floor for a moment?' – they know better,
you never get an unexpected call from that person unless …

after our conversation, which typically lasts five minutes,
they will be led out of the building by security

3

three days later, a Sunday
        and everybody is on the hill
strollers, joggers, couples, toddlers
        martial artists, readers on benches
dogs pursuing sticks and tennis balls

a blue sky criss-crossed
        with a loosely woven web of contrails
dispersing softly
high above the distant shells of concrete, steel and glass

which are quiet today
hundreds of thousands of blank screens and unoccupied desks
a security guard walks along an empty corridor
bars of light and shade shift
        through silent offices as the sun
dips westward over deepest Hampshire

up from the tube into Threadneedle Street
carved pediments
    porticos with Corinthian columns
dark suits displaying poppies
    shoulder to shoulder with those who Serve
a lunch-bar chalk-board
sandwiches, coffee, Moët & Chandon (£59)

    figures in alleys and under arches
    feed on smart-phone screens and cigarettes

past the Monument (to the Great Fire of 1666)
the better to preserve the memory of this dreadful visitation
28,196 cubic feet of Portland stone at a cost of £13,450 11s 9d
with a viewing platform at a height of 202 feet, from which

    John Cradock (a baker)
    Lyon Levi (a diamond merchant)
    Leander (a baker)
    Margaret Moyes (the daughter of a baker)
    Robert Donaldson Hawes (a fifteen-year-old boy)
    and Jane Cooper (a servant-girl)

leapt, between 1788 and 1842, to their deaths
the gallery thereafter enclosed in an iron cage

and so passing on
    to Lower Thames Street
no clatter, no chatter from within
    no pleasant whining of a mandolin
audible above the insistence of the traffic

inexplicable splendour of Ionian white and gold
closed today
we are sorry for any inconvenience

II

landscapes

The Poetry of Place

1

thistles among wheat
moor grass in a marshy place beside a canal
across a valley a village vanishes
as a shower draws a grey veil across the landscape

rain on a slate roof
an articulated lorry parked on a gravel road among puddles

level crossings
small stations on the line across the Vale of York
each with a wooden signal box (manned)
cow parsley and some yellow flowers I don't know the name of

the further west we go the heavier the rain becomes
three wet horses stand motionless in a small green paddock

2

A bosky landskip, passage through which
much delighted all the members of our party.

Mr Gray had brought with him his *Glass*,
a convex, oval mirror with a tinted surface,
with the aid of which he viewed the scene,
afterwards prevailing upon all of us to do the same.

Copses, dells and knolls
lavishly scattered by Nature's gen'rous hand –
yet the very picture of a picture
by that amiable and perfect master, Claude!

Mr Gray instructed us that,
for the glass to work as it ought,
we must turn our backs on the object we wished to view
and screen our eyes from the sun.

3

One of the country's best preserved castles, a massive
fortress with walls nine feet thick.

Built between 1378 and 1399 by Lord Richard Scrope,
treasurer and chancellor to King Richard II.

Mary Queen of Scots was imprisoned here from 1568 to
1569. Royalists were besieged here during the Civil War.

The perfect venue for private functions and corporate
events.

4

a field of lavender
a disc harrow rusting in the corner of a farmyard
a row of cabin cruisers moored along a river bank
a creosoted fence wet with sudden rain

a fishing boat, mast still erect
sunk to its gunwales in estuary mud
patches of sunlight and a gusty, salty wind
small waves hurry in over rippled sand

the tide ebbs
uncovers the masonry course by course
festoons of weed, arches in the stonework
a damp stain marks the spring tide's height

behind the quay
a street of small but handsome Georgian houses
rises to a granite church
and a monument to an 'explorer of the African continent'

a seagull wheels and cries
high over the well-appointed offices
of estate agents and land valuers, investment advisors
solicitors and commissioners for oaths

I

The typical Cornish hedge is a hybrid between a stone wall and an earthen bank with bushes or trees growing along its top. It has an earth core, faced each side with local stone, usually tapered with an inward curve from the base to half-way up.

Some still existing Cornish hedges date from the Bronze and Iron Ages, 2,000–4,000 years ago, when Cornwall's traditional pattern of landscape became established. Many other hedges resulted from mediaeval field rationalisations, and more originated in the tin-and-copper industrial boom of the eighteenth and nineteenth centuries, when heaths and uplands were enclosed. There are about 30,000 miles of hedges today.

In other parts of Britain, most early hedges were destroyed during the Saxon or Norman periods with the establishment of the open-field system. These open fields were enclosed again by the Enclosure Acts, but the hedges were then removed as a result of food shortage and mechanisation after the Second World War.

These changes tended not to happen in Cornwall, and many ancient hedges still exist. These often show, by the surviving species, the kind of habitat that used to be in their vicinity long ago, for instance, bell heather in hedges where the surrounding moorland was reclaimed, or dog's mercury and bluebells where woodland has vanished.

The population of a mile of healthy Cornish hedge would normally include specimens of between one and two hundred different flowering species; if not, it is likely that it is maintenance-damaged. This floral diversity attracts an estimated ten thousand species of insects, and their presence in turn attracts a wide variety of small mammals, birds, and reptiles who come to forage and build their nests.

2

bird's foot
     bittersweet
          white campion
night-flowering catch-fly

red clover
     hedgerow cranesbill
          ox-eye daisy
field forget-me-not

common fumitory
     purple fumitory
          tall ramping fumitory
western fumitory

goutweed
     autumnal hawkbit
          beaked hawksbeard
cross-leaved heath

early purple orchid
    fool's parsley
        field scabious
common toadflax

English stonecrop
    lesser yellow trefoil
        kidney vetch
weasel's snout

field pansy
    self-heal
        wood sorrel
common primrose

3

a peculiar whirring, smashing, clattering, destructive sound
a County Highways tractor
with a shiny new machine of a kind I had never seen before

as it lifted to avoid a telegraph pole, I glimpsed
enough to understand the way it worked

a long box-arm full of whirling flails
sucking into its maw
the tide of flowers and busy insects
smashing everything and leaving behind
nothing but a silent bank
and a thick mess like coarse lawn-mowings

I picked up a lump of the green mess
shaking it apart in the vain hope of living things emerging

with the green fragments
a shower of little crushed pieces fell
that could hardly be recognised but for an insect wing here
or a tiny head or leg there

scattered all along the road at my feet
was a mass of torn and shredded greenery and flower-heads
thickly strewn with the soft bodies of moths
many cut in half yet still pulsing
a confetti of small bright wings
crushed beetles, dead hoverflies, fragmented bees
disembowelled frogs, little bloody pieces of voles and shrews
crushed silvery bits of slow-worms
pieces of snails, pulped caterpillars
and now and then the tiny paw or tail of a field mouse

of all the scores of grasshoppers that a few moments before
had been flicking out in front of my dog
as he nosed his way along beside the verge
not one could be seen alive

I followed in the wake of the machine all the way home
stupidly trying to avoid stepping on the corpses

4

along this typical mile of Cornish lane
repeated use of the flail has caused the disappearance of about

49

90 flowering herbaceous species
5 shrub species
20 grass species
60 moss species
40 bird species
20 butterfly species
250 larger moth species
hundreds of other invertebrate species

since the last yellowhammer flew across the road in 1980
I have never seen another while walking here

since the last grasshopper in July 1981
I have never seen or heard another in these hedges

5

Italian arum (greatly increased, rampant)

hogweed (greatly increased)

ivy (vastly increased, rampant)

Japanese knotweed (greatly increased)

three-cornered leek (greatly increased, rampant)

nettle (greatly increased)

false oat-grass (rampant)

cow parsley (much increased)

rosebay willow-herb (greatly increased, rampant)

bracken (vastly increased, rampant)

AUGUST LINES

in memory of Sheila Winifred Rossiter (1925–2008)
and for Mark and Emma

31 *July* 2008

taking the express from London to York

wheat fields, hedgerows
moor grass in a marshy place beside a canal
across a valley a village smudged out
as a shower draws a veil across the landscape

rain on a slate roof
an articulated lorry parked on a gravel road among puddles
(glimpsed as we slow through Doncaster)

alight at York for all stations to Knaresborough and Harrogate
cross draughty platforms
under the high curve of the train-shed roof
to a throbbing, rattling two-coach diesel

level crossings and small stations on the branch line
each with a wooden signal box (manned)
cow parsley beside the track
and some yellow flowers I no longer know the name of

1 *August*

walk up Coppice Drive
(visits to school-friends in the long summer holidays)
and along the Ripon Road
(discovering *Encounter* in a dentist's waiting room)

past the Cairn Hydro Hotel
(a summer job washing dishes in a basement
condensation trickling down mould-blackened walls)
and past the Royal Hall

cupolas and pagoda-like towers with green copper roofs
(Emile Ford gyrating to 'Red Sails in the Sunset')
KURSAAL elegantly carved in stone above the doorway
(George Melly mugging his way through 'Frankie and Johnny')

walk through the town
seeing what memories present themselves
picking them up, looking at them from different angles
then putting them back in the places they belong

walk up The Ginnel
which really did use to be a ginnel, dark and cobbled
but which now, widened, is just another street
with a café, two bars and an over-priced antique shop

Busby's (now Debenhams) still there on the corner
Mum and a small myself – after all these years –
still having elevenses in the first-floor tea-room
one sunny morning in the 1950s

7 August

on a hilltop by a pine wood, the three of us
take turns to cradle the heavy plastic container
scatter granular grey ashes among damp bracken
beside the big stone where she liked to sit
and look out over the valley

dry-stone walls, brambles
wind bends yellowing grasses
horizon blotted out by low cloud and mist

not by any means an easy life
difficult father, mistaken marriage
martyrdom to duty, then divorce and acrimony
money worries, children brought up single-handed
lonely retirement
arthritis, fragile bones and failing sight

yes, all true –
but now, standing on the hilltop in failing light
I think I sense a different person:
optimistic, ready for anything
jaunty in her Wren's cap on the quay at Malta
in the early spring of 1945 –

> someone I never really knew
> despite that small framed photo
> on the mahogany side table in her dining room …

wind combs the frail yellow grasses
rain starts to fall

walk down from the hilltop
stop for a moment, look back, and then go on
through fields of thick grass in increasing rain

the beck in spate in the valley bottom
turbulent, dark brown
streaked yellow with mud washed down by the torrent

12 *August*

An hour spent looking through her books: Barry from the
charity shop is coming to pick them up tomorrow. In her
copy of an Open University textbook, *Culture and Society
in Britain* 1850–1890, she'd underlined a quotation from
Harriett Taylor Mill's 'Enfranchisement of Women' (1851):

*We deny the right of any portion of the species to decide for
another portion, or any individual for another individual,
what is and what is not their 'proper sphere'. The proper sphere
for all human beings is the largest and highest which they are
able to attain to.*

13 *August*, 4 A.M.

Emma in Sheffield, Mark in Sharjah
for me a last night in this flat
awake in the spare room, listening
to a wet gusty wind blowing across miles of Yorkshire

gritstone outcrops high on Blubberhouses Moor
gnarled clumps of heather on blackened stems

wind and rain and darkness
someone's sheep
huddle among cotton grass and tumbled stones
in the lee of a half-ruined dry-stone wall

13 *August*, 11:30 A.M.

John from Dublin
and the old man he's brought along to help him

boxes and boxes of stuff
heaps of now useless things from the garage
ten minutes to get the wardrobe down the stairs
the wardrobe then reduced to splinters with an axe
everything goes into the high-sided truck

will the old man survive the day?
a white-haired melancholic ancient
with watering eyes and an ashen face

occasionally he stops work
to roll a cigarette and then laboriously smoke it
stands with head bowed while he does so
perfectly still
apart from a faint shaking of the hands

13 *August*, 2 P.M.

the beck looks as it always did
grassy margins, small sandbanks
muddy gaps between trees where the cattle wade
rounded boulders embedded in the stream's smooth flow
the willow tree on whose limbs
we boys would swing out over the water
still there, fifty years older, but showing no signs of that

then on up the hill
shadowy pine wood beside me all the way
as I climb to the crest

dry-stone walls, outcrops of millstone grit
the fields fall steeply to the beck
a silver birch rustles halfway down the slope
the horizon visible today
spiky with the slow gesticulations of a wind farm

I sit on the big flat stone
to feed the living
eat my cheese-and-chutney sandwich

my last time in this place, I suppose

a peaceful place, a beautiful place
to disperse into one's final rest

no sign of any ashes after last week's rain

13 *August*, 4 P.M.

the final emptiness of the flat

closing the door on it
turning the key and walking away
waiting on the windy platform
starting on a journey to the other end of the country
beginning by passing through a cutting green with summer grasses
then out across the tall-arched viaduct

Almscliff Crag
that small knuckle of gritstone on its hilltop

> *supporting*, Andrew Marvell says,
> *the heavens on its Atlantean peak*

visible from the train as far as Wharfedale
then dropping out of sight

INSTANCES

a temple on a mountain
burnt down ten times in a thousand years

a terrace high above
a valley of steep roofs and blossoming trees

a bowl of soba and mountain vegetables
in a cobbled alley near the temple gate

a dead plum tree
another almost as ancient grows beside it

blossoms push out
through the black bark of the trunk itself

III

found in transcription

TOWNE, HAUEN & COUNTREY ADIOYNING

Richard Carew of Antony, *The Survey of Cornwall*, 1602

Saltash

is seated
on the declyning of a steep hill
consisteth of three streets
        which euery showre washeth cleane
compriseth between 80. and 100. households
vnderlyeth the gouernment of a Maior & his 10. brethren
and possesseth sundry large priuiledges ouer the whole hauen

to wit
an yeerely rent of boates and barges appertayning to the harbour
ancorage of strange shipping
crowning of dead persons, laying of arrests
and other Admirall rights

here dwelleth one *Grisling*
deafe from a long time, who hath
a strange quality to vnderstand what you say
(contrary to the rules of nature and yet without the helpe of arte)
by marking the mouing of your lips

I had almost forgotten to tell you that
there is a well in this towne
whose water
will neuer boyle peas to a seasonable softnes

Launceston

those buildings commonly knowne by the name of Launston
and written Lanceston
are by the *Cornishmen* called *Lesteeuan*
(*Lez* in *Cornish* signifieth broad, *&* those are scatteringly erected)

they are gouerned by
a Maior and his scarlet-robde brethren

there is
adioynant in site but sequestred in iurisdiction
an ancient Castle whose steepe rocky-footed Keepe
hath his top enuironed with a treble wall

and in regard thereof
men say was called

Castle Terrible

Bodmin

in *Cornish, Bos venna*
commonly termed Bodman
which (by illusion if not Etimology)
a man might not vnaptly turne into Badham
for of all the townes in Cornwall I hold
none more contagiously seated than this

it consisteth wholly of one street
whose South side is hidden from the Sunne by an high hill
so neerly coasting it in most places as neither can
light haue entrance to their staires
nor open ayre to their other roomes

their back houses
of more necessary than cleanly seruice
as kitchins, stables, &c.
are clymed up vnto by steps, and their filth
by euery great showre
washed downe through their houses into the streetes

Tintagel

more famous for his antiquite
than regardable for his present estate

(yet the ruines
argue it to haue been once
no vnworthie dwelling for the *Cornish* princes)

halfe the buildings
were raised on the continent and
the other halfe on an Iland

in passing thither
you must first descend with a dangerous declyning
and then make a worse ascent by a path
through his sticklenesse occasioning
and through his steepnesse threatning
the ruine of your life with the failing of your foote

at the top
two or three terrifying steps giue you
entrance to the hill
which supplieth pasture for sheepe and conyes

Padstow

a towne and hauen of sutable quality
for both (though bad)
are the best that the north *Cornish* coast possesseth

the harbor is barred with banks of sand
made (through vniting their weake forces)
sufficiently strong to resist
the Ocean's threatning billows
which (diuorced from their parent)
find their rage subdued
by the other's lowly submission

Mr *Nicholas Prideaux* from his new
and stately house thereby
taketh a ful and large prospect of
the towne, hauen *&* countrey adioyning

to all which his wisdome is a stay
his authority a direction

Wadebridge

the salt water leaving Padstowe
floweth vp into the countrey that it may
embrace the riuer Camel, and
hauing performed this naturall courtesie
ebbeth away againe to yield him the freer passage

by which meanes
they both vndergoe Wade bridge
the longest, strongest and fayrest that the Shire can muster

Lostwithiel

Maioralty, markets, faires
and nomination of Burgesses for the parliament
it hath common with the most

Coynage of Tynne
onely with three others
but the gayle for the whole
Stannary and keeping of the County Courts
it selfe alone

yet all this can hardly
rayse it to a tolerable condition of wealth and inhabitance

wherefore I will detayne you no longer

THE CORNISH HOUSE

Richard Carew of Antony, *The Survey of Cornwall*, 1602

I

the ancient maner of *Cornish* building was
    whereas now-adayes they
to plant their houses lowe
    seat their dwellings high
to lay the stones with morter of lyme and sand
    lay them with earthen morter
to make the walles thick
    build their walles thinne
to make their windowes arched and little
    mould their lights large
to frame the roomes not to exceed two stories
    raise them to three or foure stoaries
seeking therethrough onely strength and warmnesse
    coueting chiefly prospect and pleasure

2

for covering of Houses, there are three sorts of Slate
the first and best, Blew:
in substance thinne, in colour faire
in waight light, in lasting strong

the Sea strond also in many places affordeth
Peebble-stones, which
are by often rolling of the waues wrought to a kind of roundnesse
and serue verie handsomely for pauing of streetes and Courts

3

the poore Cotagers content themselues with
Cob for their wals and Thatch for their couering
few partitions, no planchings or glasse windows
and scarcely any chimnies
other then a hole in the wall to let out the smoke

straw and blanket
a mazer and a panne or two comprise all their substance

The Invention *of the* Lake District

Thomas Gray to Dr Thomas Wharton, 1769

I

walk'd over a spungy meadow or two
& began to mount the hill thro' a broad
& straight green alley among the trees
& with some toil gained the summit
& from hence saw the Lake majestic in its calmness, clear
& smooth as a blew mirror with winding shores
& low points of land cover'd with green inclosures
& white farm houses looking out among the trees
& cattle feeding

descended again by a side avenue
& continued my way along the shore, close to the water
& generally on a level with it
& saw a cormorant flying over it
& fishing

2

our path tends here to the left
& the ground gently rising
& cover'd with a glade of scattering trees
& bushes on the very margin of the water

then opens both ways the most
delicious view, that my eyes ever beheld

behind you are the magnificent heights of *Walla*-crag
& opposite lie the thick hanging woods of Ld Egremont
& *Newland*-valley with green
& smiling fields embosom'd in the dark cliffs
& to the left the jaws of *Borodale*
& that chaos of mountain behind mountain roll'd in confusion
& beneath you the shining purity of the *Lake*, ruffled by the breeze
& reflecting rocks, woods, fields
& inverted tops of mountains
& with the white buildings of *Keswick*, *Crosthwaite*-church
& *Skiddaw* for a back-ground at distance

oh Doctor!

I never wish'd more for you – & pray think
how the glass played its part in such a spot!

3

soon after we came under *Gowder*-crag
a hill more formidable to the eye
& to the apprehension than that of *Lodoor*

the rocks atop
deep-cloven perpendicularly by the rains, hanging loose
& nodding forwards, seem just starting from their base in shivers

the whole way down
the road on both sides is strew'd with piles of the fragments
strangely thrown across each other
& of dreadful bulk

the place reminds one of those passes in the Alps
where the Guides tell you to move on with speed
& say nothing
lest the agitation of the air should loosen the snows above
& bring down a mass, that would overwhelm a caravan

I took their counsel and hasten'd on in silence
non ragioniam di lor; ma guarda, e passa

4

in the evening walk'd alone down to the lake
by the side of *Crow-Park* after sunset

& saw the solemn covering of night draw on
the last gleam of sunshine fading away on the hill-tops
the deep serene of the waters
& the long shadows of the mountains thrown across them
till they nearly touch'd the hithermost shore

at distance heard the murmur
of many waterfalls not audible in the day-time

wish'd for the Moon, but she was
dark to me & silent, hid in her vacant interlunar cave

5

the road in some parts made, in others
dangerous for carriages, slippery
& stony, but no precipices

a very beautiful view down the Lake

the inhabitants pronounce the name
of *Skiddaw-fell* with a sort of terror and aversion

a little to the west a stone bridge of 3 arches
here I dined at an inn that stands there

the sky was overcast
& the wind cool

several little showers today

said to be snow on *Cross-fell*

6

from the shore a low promontory pushes itself far into the water
& on it stands the white village of *Grasmere*
with the parish-church rising in the middle of it

hanging inclosures
corn-fields
& meadows as green as an emerald with their trees
& hedges
& cattle
fill up the whole space from the edge of the water
& just opposite to you is a large farmhouse
at the bottom of a steep smooth lawn embosom'd in old woods
wch climb half-way up the mountain's side
& discover above them a broken line of crags, that crown the scene

not a single red tile
no flaring Gentleman's house
or garden walls
break in upon the repose of this little unsuspected paradise
all is peace, beauty
& happy poverty in its neatest most becoming attire

Words by Samuel Palmer & His Son Herbert

Samuel Palmer's eldest son, Thomas More Palmer, died in 1861 at the age of 19; after Palmer's own death in 1881, his younger son, Alfred Herbert Palmer, wrote and edited *The Life and Letters of Samuel Palmer, Painter and Etcher*, published in London in 1892.

1

outlines cannot be got too black

we must not begin with medium
but think always on excess
and only use medium to make excess more abundantly excessive

we are not troubled with aerial perspective in the valley of vision

whatever you do guard against bleakness and grandeur
and try for the primitive cottage feeling

2

a certain sentiment of surpassing fruitfulness

if nature has been consulted
it has been consulted as it were in a distorting glass

a huge bank of cumulus clouds which look
(as Mr Hook says of the cumuli of Cadore)
as if you could knock your head against them

bright crimson apples so numerous and so enormous
as far to surpass the utmost stretch of possibility
a tremendous and utterly abnormal crop

bits of nature are generally much improved by being received
$$\text{into the soul}$$

he could not have passed the most absurdly elementary examination
in botany, entomology, ornithology, or geology

exhibitions
of clover and beans and parsley and mushrooms and cow dung
and the innumerable etceteras of a foreground

3

a nice tight armful of a spirited young lady

Italy
especially Rome
is quite a new world

I can never paint in my old style again

4

today the first snow has fallen on our dear boy's grave

what is called a beautiful view gives me
no more real pleasure than the contemplation

of a kitchen sink

5

forswear HOLLOW compositions like Calypso and St Paul
and forswear great spaces of sky

TAKE SHELTER in TREES

an almost feminine want of reticence
in matters relating to his feelings, griefs and disappointments

Thursday, rose without much horror

a living inhumement
and equal to the dread throes of suffocation, turning
this valley of vision into a fen of scorpions and stripes and agonies

MISERABLY HAMPERED

though nobody will believe it
because I am round in the waist
and the corners of my mouth turn up naturally

Yours affectionately, The Most Unhappy of Men, S. Palmer

Piet Mondrian in Belsize Park

Letters (1938-1940) from 60 Parkhill Road, NW3, to
Winifred Nicholson in Cumberland, and (after 1939)
to Ben Nicholson and Barbara Hepworth in St Ives.

I

I am always glad to be here!
the air is good for my health but above all
the spiritual surroundings here is better than in Paris to me

2

I have difficulty with an ear and the nose
Dr Coburg took wax out of one of them but
a noise remains in the other

and then the nose began to be wrong
one nose hole is too narrow and already 20 years ago
I suffered with it

3

haven't you suffered of the cold?
I only a few days by that great wind

after the snow falling the heating is sufficient
against such a wind is nothing

4

my work goes better than ever

5

Mr Morton
made the impression on me as if there was no war at all

that was a little strange to me
I think one must suffer when all are suffering

perhaps Mr Morton is too young to me

6

I am so late to answer you because
I had so much to do

only making the black-out with little costs
took me 2 weeks

.

7

even I began a new composition (small)

and also an article in relation with the world situation:
'Art Shows the Evil of Totalitarian Tendencies'

perhaps it may be of use

8

since Paris fell
I did no more creative work

the day is too near

might the Nazis come in, what then?
my article won't do me much good, neither

9

I am trying to get a visa to New York

I should have liked to see you before
but I don't think I succeed with getting out
it will be too late

10

I have not lost confidence in Human's future
and Progress

and for we make part of that Progress
perhaps we will overcome the darkness

11

I suffered from intestines-troubles caused by the liver
every week I was at the doctor
nearly better
I got a little fishbone in the throat that bothered me much

then my windows were blown in
(fortunately I had my black-out
but shutters were blown half open all the same!)
by a bomb a little farther in Parkhill rd

I was on bed but had only dust in an eye

lucky!

12

yesterday I took my valises
out up here in Ormonde-Hôtel where I stay
untill I go

here there is a good shelter under the hôtel

I do like your photo of relief
only I should like the big round a little otherwise placed
it goes to the left

your old friend Mondrian

I believe in our end victory!

IV

ars longa

Mary Celeste

a text abandoned by

almost in the middle of

the language not entirely

the sentences strangely

the words show no signs of

we find ourselves unable to

the silence is undeniably

the page has been laid out as if

HOMAGE TO WCW

weeds and leafless vines
scattered

brownish
no signs of life

what's to be done with
all this verbiage?

the doctor
drives past the field

on his way to
the contagious hospital

the words, rooted
grip down, begin to awaken

ARS POETICA

languaged
moving through

affected by
and affecting

a locale (itself
always in transition)

noticing what's there
asking to be noticed

shaping the traces
into an asymmetrical

pleasing verbal object
that can stand on

its own feet – however
many there turn out to be –

the shaping
of the language being

the shaping of the world
that shapes the self

that shapes the world that
shapes the poem

By Whole Cartloads

an ensemble of instances

a stenography of the immediate

    the diary shapes the life

I believe in the coherent work with many voices

    eye sees, sun shines
    footslog, you want arguments too?

the pageant begins
and the stuff by whole cartloads comes in

Quotations from Tony Baker (two), Laurie Duggan, Octavio Paz, Alan Halsey, and Thomas Nashe.

As Far As

I can
remember
once

I have
started
painting

I am
occupied
mainly

with
putting
things

in the
right
place

Statement by William Coldstream (1908–1987).

Bonfire of the Adjectives

fear adjectives; they bleed nouns (Basil Bunting)

arched arched
bald
belabouring
black
blue
bored
bristling
ceaseless
cool
curling
clustered
dark dark
deep deep deep deep
deft
detached
discarded
domed
driven
early early
feathered
fledged
frozen
gleaming
glowing
great
green
grey
grey-green

huge huge
knobbly
long long
nippled
overwhelmed
pale
reliable
responsible
salty
scrubbed
scruffy
sharp
silent
small small small
squeaky
steel-clad
swift
tempered
territorial
tiny
toothed
tree-lined
tusked
unimpeded
unsuffering
white white
worn
yellow yellow

safely removed from twenty-six older poems, January 2013

These Be the Words

he fucks you up, that Larkin bloke
he means to and he does it well
palming off his self-dislike
as every living person's hell

he was fucked up too of course
before he sat down at his desk
to give diminishment a voice
and re-write life as Larkinesque

he spreads his misery far and wide
it's bad for everybody's health
stop reading him is my advice
and never write such stuff yourself

V

white foxglove

1 *The goddess of Shaman Mountain*

in a fold of the mountains
wearing a coat of fig-leaves and a rabbit-floss girdle
a cloak of stone-orchids with a belt of wild ginger
in a car of lily-magnolia with a banner of woven cassia
driving tawny leopards and leading striped lynxes
the lady of the mountains is fragrant with pollia

clouds in the morning, rain in the evening
she drinks from rocky springs beneath the pine trees
thunder rumbles, rain darkens the sky
monkeys chatter and apes scream in the night

2 *Pollia japonica*

herbs perennial
stems erect or ascending, puberulent
leaf sheaths glabrous
leaf blade narrowly elliptic
cincinni numerous, often in several whorls, some in panicles
bracts membranous
sepals ovate-orbicular, glabrous, persistent
petals white, obovate-spatulate
six stamens, all fertile, fruit globose
fl. Jul–Sep, fr. Sep–Oct

forests in ravines
near sea level to 1200 m

Hoping to Trigger the End of Neo-Liberalism by Going for a Walk

the very notion of 'landscape' seems to induce an effect of smoothing; the very fact of visual continuity implies a kind of present reconciliation (Patrick Keiller)

I

perfectly still, no tracking, panning or zooming
the camera opens its eye
      on a field of yellow oilseed rape
we sit and watch the wind as it goes about its business

a meadow containing
browsing cows and an iron valve
(underground pipeline to an American Airforce base)

white foxglove swaying
bees visit hedgerow flowers in drowsy sunshine
a spider meticulously attends to its web
bird-twitter, insect-buzz, leaves ruffle in the breeze

car factory, early-warning tracking station
Atomic Weapons Establishment (AWE)
just out of shot
over the next hill

an even-toned voice-over

> *the Government Pipeline and Storage System comprises about 2,500 kilometres of pipeline and forty-six depots, eleven of which are still in use, moving about five billion litres of fuel every year*

Patrick Keiller, *Robinson in Ruins*

supposedly
nineteen rusting cans of film
found abandoned in a derelict caravan

2

a rising of the people to pulle downe the enclosures
but for himself happ what would
for he could die but once and
he would not alwaies live like a slave
Bartholomew Steer
tortured, died in Newgate Prison, 1597

at Otmoor in 1830
protestors against the enclosure of the wetland common
destroyed every fence and hedge that they encountered
while in Berkshire and Oxfordshire
threatening letters, meetings, riots
rick-burning, the destruction of machines,
rioters marching from farm to farm demanding
food and drink and higher wages
101 gaoled, 58 transported, 27 sentenced to death

nature, pastoral, picturesque
'landscape' saturated with conflicted histories

and now in the twenty-first century
a new machine moves, indifferent, relentless
across the flat brown earth, ploughing
while gulls take advantage of the moment

you would never know . . .

a satellite ground station on Enslow Hill
where Robert Burton and Richard Bradshaw
        Bartholomew Steer's companions
were hanged, drawn and quartered

3

at Westcott
from 1946
the Rocket Propulsion Establishment
        (top secret, never marked on maps)
staffed by German scientists and technicians
German weapons on-site for study

        v-1 flying bomb
        v-2 rocket
        Feuerlilie f-55 subsonic missile
        Messerschmidt me-163 rocket-propelled interceptor
        Rheintochter-1 anti-aircraft missile
        Ruhrstahl x-4 air-to-air wire-controlled missile

preparing the ground for
Black Arrow, Waxwing, Black Knight, Jaguar, Skylark, Sea Slug
privatised in 1987 (British Aerospace)

to the west raf Brize Norton
to the south Henry 'Hangman' Hawley's house
        the troops dread his severity, hate the man and
        hold his military knowledge in contempt
to the east the disused quarry and former cement works
in the parish of Chinnor

a multitude of alehouses
a check to industry and good order

enclosure of the commons attempted
1761, 1817, 1847, at last successful in 1854

268 lace-makers
including labourers' wives and 86 children

Chinnor, dormitory village for
Thame, High Wycombe, Aylesbury and London
still has a lace group

4

biophilia
the camera lingers on wild flowers

      white foxglove swaying
      bees visit hedgerow flowers in drowsy sunshine

narrative suspended
long moments
spent in a world without *Homo sapiens*

non-human intelligences
      the lichen *Xanthoria parietina*, for example
mute heralds of a future without humanity
      (lichen already the dominant
      life form over large areas of Earth)

The Possibility of Life's Survival on the Planet
(Tate Publishing, 16 Mar 2012, hardcover, £12.99)

a spider meticulously attends to its web

> *it seems to be easier for us today to imagine the thorough-going deterioration of the earth and of nature than the breakdown of late capitalism – perhaps that is due to some weakness in our imagination* (Frederic Jameson)

bird-twitter
insect-buzz
leaves ruffle in the breeze

we sit and watch the machine as it goes about its business

Near Porthcothan

cottages on a sandy lane
a padlocked shop
a path through tamarisks to a headland

blue sky and running seas
deep Atlantic swell
offshore islands swathed in avalanches of spray

a beach at the base of granite cliffs
rock-stacks, tide-rippled sand
the sea fuming and roiling

a church by an abandoned runway
a village demolished for a 1940s airbase
acres of unkempt grassland

a narrow valley ablaze with gorse
a plank bridge
reed beds and hoofed-up muddy places

the shallow stream
empties itself
over a shingle beach into the ocean

notes & sources

NOTES & SOURCES

These poems were written between 2008 and 2015; many thanks to Chris Cleary, Andrew Fitzsimons, John Gribble and Lesley Hardy, who commented on earlier versions. Japanese names appear in the Japanese order, with the family name first.

§

READING PHILIP WHALEN 'Since You Ask Me', and 'Plum, Metaphysics, an Investigation, a Visit, and a Short Funeral Ode' (in *On Bear's Head*, 1969); '7.III.67' (in *Severance Pay*, 1970); and Michael McClure, *Scratching the Beat Surface*, 1982.

REMEMBERING LOL COXHILL Lol Coxhill (1932–2012): British soprano-saxophonist, busker, raconteur and festival compère.

BEING IN TUNE i.m. Stan Tracey (30 December 1926–6 December 2013): pianist, composer and band-leader, a key figure in British jazz from the 1950s onwards. The Bull's Head is a London pub which has been presenting modern jazz since 1959.

RECOMMENDING TRISTANO Richard Cook and Brian Morton, *The Penguin Guide to Jazz Recordings* (9th ed., 2008); Larry Kart, liner notes to *The Complete Atlantic Recordings of Lennie Tristano, Lee Konitz & Warne Marsh* (Mosaic, 1997); J. Bradford Robinson, article on Tristano in *The New Grove Dictionary of Jazz* (1994); Barry Ulanov, liner notes to *The New Tristano* (Atlantic, 1961).

KNOWING ONE'S PLACE Setagaya Hachiman Shrine, Gōtokuji Temple and what remains of Setagaya Castle are all within a few yards of each other in Miyanosaka in Setagaya Ward, a residential area of southwest Tokyo. The castle, seat of the Kira clan, was destroyed by Toyotomi Hideyoshi (1536/37–1598) after his defeat of the Hōjō clan, with whom the Kira were allied, at the siege of Odawara in 1590. At Sekigahara in 1600 the successors of Hideyoshi were in turn defeated by Tokugawa Ieyasu (1543–1616) in a battle that was instrumental in establishing Ieyasu as undisputed ruler of Japan; the rule of his family lasted until the Meiji Restoration of 1868. The treaty signed by Ii Naosuke was an unequal one, opening Japanese ports and granting extraterritorial privileges to American citizens, hence the resentment of it.

KNOWING ONE'S PLACE: PART 2 The first quotation in italics is from an eighteenth-century official of the Bakufu (shogunate). Until the Meiji Restoration only aristocrats and samurai were allowed to have family names.

VISITING THE ANCESTORS Taisho Era, 1912–1926; *okonomiyaki*, a savoury pancake containing a variety of ingredients (*okonomi* = what you like, *yaki* = grilled); *shōchū*, a Japanese distilled drink; NHK, the Japanese national broadcasting corporation; *half*, Japanese English for a person of mixed race; the Heike (also known as the Taira), one of the clans (opposed by the Genji/Minamoto clan) fighting for control of Japan in the Genpei war of 1180–1185, a struggle recounted in the epic *Heike Monogatari* (The Tale of the Heike), in which the death of Taira no Atsumori is one of the most famous episodes; *dera*, a temple; *sakaki*, a sacred evergreen plant.

LOOKING AT THE CITY FROM PARLIAMENT HILL Part 2: A human resources specialist talking to Joris Luyendijk over a glass of Haut Poitou Sauvignon Blanc; *The Guardian*, 2 November 2011.

THE CORNISH HEDGE Much of this piece is adapted from Sarah Carter's twenty-five year diary of a mile of hedge near her home in the West Penwith area of western Cornwall, 'The Life and Death of a Flailed Cornish Hedge' (© Sarah Carter, 2008), which can be found in the Cornish Hedges Library at www.cornishhedges.co.uk/papers.htm

AUGUST LINES *Fulcit Atlanteo rupes ea vertice caelos*: Andrew Marvell's Latin poem on Almscliff Crag and Bilborough is titled 'Epigramma in Duos Montes Amosclivium et Bilboreum', and was written in the 1650s at Appleton House in Wharfedale, where Marvell was employed by Sir Thomas Fairfax as a tutor for his daughter.

THE INVENTION OF THE LAKE DISTRICT Thomas Gray visited the Lake District for the second time in 1769. His companion, Dr Thomas Wharton, who had asthma, dropped out at Brough, early in the journey; Gray continued on his own and kept a detailed journal for the benefit of his friend. The 'glass' in part 2 is a Claude glass, a small convex mirror with a tinted surface, used by travellers to frame and view the landscape; see part 2 of 'The Poetry of Place' on pages 43–44 . The quotation at the end of part 3 is from Dante (*Inferno* 3.1.51): 'Let us not speak of them; but look and pass on.'

PIET MONDRIAN IN BELSIZE PARK Mondrian left from Liverpool for New York on 23 September 1940.

GAO-TANG The first section is adapted from parts of David Hawkes's translation of *Shan gui* ('The Mountain Spirit'), by a southern Chinese poet, possibly Qu Yuan (*c.* 249–278 BCE). According to Hawkes, the central character, who is unnamed in the poem, is probably a fertility goddess, 'the Lady of Gao-tang', goddess of Shaman Mountain (Wu-shan) above the Yangtze gorges near the eastern border of Sichuan (*The Songs of the South*, 1985). The second section draws on the article on *Pollia japonica* in the list 'Flora of China' at www.eFloras.org

HOPING TO TRIGGER THE END OF NEO-CAPITALISM BY GOING FOR A WALK Patrick Keiller, *Robinson in Ruins* (DVD, 2010); Patrick Keiller, *The Possibility of Life's Survival on the Planet* (2012) (where the phrase used as the title of the poem appears); Mark Fisher, 'English Pastoral: *Robinson in Ruins*' (*Sight & Sound*, 2010); Frederic Jameson, *The Seeds of Time* (1996); Doreen Massey, 'Landscape/Space/Politics: An Essay' (2011); Patrick Keiller, Doreen Massey and Patrick Wright, *The Future of Landscape and the Moving Image*, thefutureoflandscape.wordpress.com

www.ingramcontent.com/pod-product-compliance
Lightning Source LLC
Chambersburg PA
CBHW020919090426
42736CB00008B/706